1,000,000 Books

are available to read at

www.ForgottenBooks.com

Read online
Download PDF
Purchase in print

ISBN 978-0-265-07814-3
PIBN 10948876

For support please visit www.forgottenbooks.com

1 MONTH OF
FREE
READING

at
www.ForgottenBooks.com

By purchasing this book you are
eligible for one month membership to
ForgottenBooks.com, giving you
unlimited access to our entire
collection of over 1,000,000 titles via
our web site and mobile apps.

To claim your free month visit:
www.forgottenbooks.com/free948876

English
Français
Deutsche
Italiano
Español
Português

www.forgottenbooks.com

Mythology Photography **Fiction**
Fishing Christianity **Art** Cooking
Essays Buddhism Freemasonry
Medicine **Biology** Music **Ancient
Egypt** Evolution Carpentry Physics
Dance Geology **Mathematics** Fitness
Shakespeare **Folklore** Yoga Marketing
Confidence Immortality Biographies
Poetry **Psychology** Witchcraft
Electronics Chemistry History **Law**
Accounting **Philosophy** Anthropology
Alchemy Drama Quantum Mechanics
Atheism Sexual Health **Ancient History**
Entrepreneurship Languages Sport
Paleontology Needlework Islam
Metaphysics Investment Archaeology
Parenting Statistics Criminology
Motivational

FOREIGN CROPS and MARKETS

UNITED STATES DEPARTMENT OF AGRICULTURE
OFFICE OF FOREIGN AGRICULTURAL RELATIONS
WASHINGTON, D. C.

Vol. 41   September 9, 1940   No. 10

IN THIS ISSUE

L A T E   C A B L E S

Wheat harvesting Canadian Prairie Provinces delayed in Manitoba
and eastern Saskatchewan during week ended September 4 by general rains
but advanced in western Saskatchewan and most of Alberta under favorable
weather conditions. In Manitoba cutting practically completed and threshing about half finished. Grades somewhat lowered by recent rains. About
80 percent of wheat cut in Saskatchewan and about 25 percent threshed.
Around two-thirds of crop expected to grade No. 1 Northern but quality
somewhat lowered in the northeastern district by frost damage. In Alberta,
about 75 percent of grain cut; combining and threshing under way. Early
returns indicate high yields and good quality. Slight damage from light
frosts reported in Peace River district.

- - - - - - -

Brazil declared exports of Brazil nuts to the United States from
Para during August, 4,250 short tons unshelled and 850 short tons shelled.

- - - - - - -

Beginning October 1, 1940, Japanese weavers of cotton, rayon staple
fiber, and woolen textiles will be required to use a mixture of 20 to 30
percent of silk. This measure was intended by the Japanese Government to
increase domestic consumption of raw silk from about 400,000 bales (of 132
pounds) to 500,000 bales annually.

N O T I C E - The supplement, "United States Foreign Trade in Agricultural
Products, 1939-40," is ready for distribution and will be mailed only upon
request.

G R A I N S

AUSTRALIAN WHEAT
PROSPECTS REDUCED . . .

The 1940-41 Australian wheat crop has been suffering from below-normal rainfall practically ever since seeding began last May, according to information received in the Office of Foreign Agricultural Relations. The fields sown earliest in the season were retarded by dry weather, germination of later seedings was patchy, and late sowings were delayed. Unless good soaking rains are soon received, it is reported that a large part of the crop will be damaged beyond recovery. For this season, at least, it appears that nature has solved the question of acreage restriction, which has been under consideration by Government authorities since stocks of wheat became burdensome last year. High fertilizer prices and difficulties experienced by many farmers in obtaining loans for seed purchases have also been instrumental in controlling wheat expansion.

With a carry-over on December 1, 1939, of about 20 million bushels of wheat and production estimated at 210 million, a little short of the record crop in 1932-33, storage facilities in Australia during the 1939-40 marketing season were considerably overtaxed (see Foreign Crops and Markets for March 9, 1940). Although sales by the Australian Wheat Board from December through the middle of July are said to have been in the neighborhood of 120 million bushels, only about 60 million bushels appear to have been shipped abroad. It seems likely that the carry-over on November 30, 1940, will be three or four times as large as a year earlier, especially since it will include some quantities sold to the United Kingdom but not shipped.

In this connection, the attention of the authorities has been directed toward increasing domestic consumption. It is anticipated that larger quantities of wheat can be utilized for feeding purposes, particularly by the pig and poultry producers. Consequently, wheat below the f.a.q. standard, or affected by weevils, is being sold by the Board to such feeders at a reduced price. In recent years, it is estimated that about 8 million bushels of wheat have been used annually for feed.

- - - - - - -

UNITED STATES WHEAT-EXPORT
SEASON MAKES POOR START . . .

Exports of wheat, including flour as grain, during July, the first month of the 1940-41 marketing season, totaled only 3,686,000 bushels as compared with 7,270,000 and 12,764,000 bushels, respectively, in July 1939 and 1938. The most significant changes noted this July were the decline in exports to Europe and the percentage increase in shipments to Far Eastern markets.

UNITED STATES: Exports of wheat, including flour, to principal countries of destination, July 1938-1940

Country of destination	July					
	Exports			Percentage of total		
	1938	1939	1940	1938	1939	1940
	1,000 bushels	1,000 bushels	1,000 bushels	Percent	Percent	Percent
United Kingdom..........	4,224	1,211	1,110	33.1	16.7	30.1
Ireland.................	294	296	0	2.3	4.1	0.0
Netherlands.............	2,503	533	0	19.6	7.3	.0
Belgium.................	1,708	646	0	13.4	8.9	.0
Greece..................	308	17	0	2.4	0.2	.0
Other Europe............	1,526	123	5	12.0	1.7	.1
Total Europe..........	10,563	2,826	1,115	82.8	38.9	30.2
Costa Rica..............	55	60	39	0.4	.8	1.1
Guatemala...............	43	49	27	.3	.7	.7
Honduras................	20	30	22	.2	.4	.6
Nicaragua...............	17	26	16	.1	.4	.4
Panama..................	44	45	35	.4	.6	1.0
Panama Canal Zone.......	29	23	14	.1	.3	.4
El Salvador.............	43	41	5	.3	.6	.1
Cuba....................	496	503	262	3.9	7.0	7.1
Mexico..................	1	69	4	.0	.9	.1
Dominican Republic......	19	27	19	.2	.4	.5
Haiti...................	27	45	39	.2	.6	1.1
Bolivia.................	a/	1	1	.0	.0	.0
Brazil..................	3	16	21	.0	.2	.6
Colombia................	44	90	3	.4	1.2	.1
Ecuador.................	1	60	5	.0	.8	.1
Peru....................	9	7	9	.1	.1	.2
Venezuela...............	124	173	166	1.0	2.4	4.5
Other Latin America b/...	a/	0	0	.0	.0	.0
Total Latin America.....	975	1,265	687	7.6	17.4	18.6
West Indies c/..........	131	39	48	1.0	.5	1.3
Orient d/	65	2,486	1,290	.5	34.2	35.0
Philippine Islands.......	273	321	452	2.1	4.4	12.3
British West Africa......	40	27	25	.3	.4	.7
Others..................	717	306	69	5.7	4.2	1.9
Total..................	12,764	7,270	3,686	100.0	100.0	100.0

Compiled from official records, Bureau of Foreign and Domestic Commerce.
a/ Less than 500 bushels. b/ Argentina, Chile, Paraguay, and Uruguay.
c/ British, French, and Netherlands West Indies. d/ China, Japan, Hong Kong, and Kwantung.

    July exports to the United Kingdom, the only European market now open to United States wheat, were about one fourth as large as in 1938 and somewhat smaller than in 1939. Other European countries accounted for less than 1 percent of the total in contrast to almost 50 percent in July 1938. Latin American countries took a slightly larger percentage

of the first month's total this season, but Brazil and Peru were the
only countries of that group to which United States wheat actually moved
in larger volume, and the increase was not great. Exports to Chinese
and Japanese markets were only about half as large as in July 1939, but
accounted for a larger share of the total. The Philippine Islands was
the only market to which the United States sent a significantly larger
amount of wheat this July, as compared with the past two seasons, and
it was all in the form of flour.

- - - - - - -

JAPAN MAY IMPORT WHEAT
THIS SEASON . . . . . .

    The 1940 Japanese wheat crop, officially estimated at 61,308,000
bushels, is expected to be revised downward, according to a radiogram
from the United States agricultural attache at Shanghai, and some importation of wheat is possible as a result of reduced rice supplies.
Stocks of domestic wheat in late August were reported to be very low, but
about 60,000 tons of foreign wheat were on hand. Although prospects for
sales of United States wheat were reported to be promising, at competitive
prices with Australian, foreign-exchange restrictions will continue to
limit the quantity of wheat imported. An additional purchase of 4,000 tons
of Australian wheat is said to have been recently negotiated, part of which
is to go to Tientsin. The official price for standard domestic wheat at
the mill remained at 12.74 yen per picul ($1.35 per bushel). Foreign quo-
tations on August 1 were as follows, import duty and landing charges included: Canadian No. 1, $1.20 per bushel, No. 3, $1.14; Australian f.a.q.,
$1.13; and Manchurian, $1.70.

    Japanese flour mills in late August were busy grinding new-crop
domestic wheat. All flour distribution was put under the control of the
Central Wheat Flour Distribution Control Board on August 20. Distribution will be made by the Board, by designated prefectural governors, or
through local flour organizations to be appointed by the prefectural governors. Mills may sell their flour only through the designated organizations, and other large dealers in flour are required to sell their stocks
to the Government. The Ministry of Agriculture must approve the manufacture of any product in which flour is used. Until the new distribu-
ting system is worked out, certain flour mills will function in place of
the control agencies to be appointed. Wholesale prices of flour were
unchanged at $1.31 per bag; c.i.f. Dairen, $1.41; c.i.f. Tangku, $1.62
per bag.

    In the absence of official trade returns during the last months
of the season, imports of wheat into Japan during July-June 1939-40 are
still estimated at 6,016,000 bushels, most of which originated in
Australia (see Foreign Crops and Markets, August 25, 1940). Official

- - - - - - -

trade returns of flour exports, however, for April-June increased the
season's total to 3,071,000 barrels instead of 2,862,000 barrels as estimated by the Shanghai office. About two-thirds went to Manchuria and one-
third to China.

JAPAN: Exports of wheat flour by principal country of destination,
        average 1931-32 to 1935-36, annual 1936-37 to 1939-40

July-June	Manchuria a/	China	Others	Total
	1,000 barrels	1,000 barrels	1,000 barrels	1,000 barrels
Average 1931-32 to 1935-36...	2,414	368	110	2,892
1936-37........	853	10	122	985
1937-38........	1,105	1,817	28	2,950
1938-39........	1,922	409	1	2,332
1939-40........	2,054	1,016	1	3,071

Compiled from official trade returns. a/ Includes Kwantung Leased Ter-
ritory.

- - - - - - -

URUGUAYAN CROPS SUFFERED
FROM ADVERSE WEATHER
IN 1939-40 . . . . . .

        The final official estimates for 1939-40 of the most important
cereal crops of Uruguay show a reduction from the previous year, except
in the case of flaxseed. All suffered from adverse weather and plant
diseases. Wheat declined by about 7 percent in acreage and 36 percent in
production, and some importation has been necessary in order to cover domestic requirements until 1940-41 wheat is available. The oat crop was
about 23 percent smaller than in the previous year and somewhat below
average. Barley on the other hand, while slightly below the 1938-39 out-
turn, was considerably above average. The acreages sown to both crops
were smaller than in 1938-39 but above average.

URUGUAY: Acreage and production of specified crops, average
          1933-34 to 1937-38, annual 1938-39 to 1939-40

Crop	Average 1933-34 to 1937-38		1938-39		1939-40	
	Acreage	Production	Acreage	Production	Acreage	Production
	1,000 acres	1,000 bushels	1,000 acres	1,000 bushels	1,000 acres	1,000 bushels
Wheat.........	1,183	13,252	1,256	15,461	1,165	9,901
Oats.........	202	2,917	245	3,589	215	2,764
Barley........	26	394	41	638	35	520
Flaxseed......	332	3,205	452	4,425	584	5,296

Compiled from official sources.

There has been a marked expansion in flaxseed production in recent years. Large crops were obtained in 1930 and 1931, but a sharp reduction occurred in 1932, and the 1939-40 harvest was the first to exceed 5 million bushels since 1930. The gain has resulted almost entirely from increased acreage; yields per acre have not been any higher than in earlier years.

A law of May 25, 1940, authorized the Uruguayan Ministry of Agriculture to grant seed loans to farmers during 1940 for their wheat, corn, anf flax crops. A further decree of August 8 stipulated that such loans could be repaid by the farmers in seed of their own harvesting if of the same variety as the seed loaned to them. No farmer is to receive more than 5,000 kilograms (about 11,000 pounds) of wheat seed, but those having an early variety may exchange for a later one, even though the former may have been purchased privately. Imports of seed wheat may enter the country free of duty until October 15, and the Government will aid the farmers to obtain the use of agricultural implements, in order that seeding may be hastened. It is expected that all official institutions having warehouses will place them at the disposal of the Ministry, and the Bank of the Republic is to provide the necessary funds to carry out these measures.

- - - - - - -

PERU PROHIBITS RYE IMPORTS . . .

The Peruvian Government, by decrees issued July 9 and 19, prohibited the importation of rye and rye flour and assumed control of trade in rye and quinua (an indigenous grain) destined for baking purposes, according to information received in the Office of Foreign Agricultural Relations. These decrees were made in order to supplement an earlier measure that made compulsory the mixing of rye and quinua flour with all flour made from imported wheat (see Foreign Crops and Markets, August 12, 1940). It is hoped by the local authorities that these measures will be effective in preventing speculation, in protecting domestic producers from foreign competition, and in adjusting rye and quinua prices to regional costs of production.

- - - - - - -

UNITED STATES RICE EXPORTS
AND SHIPMENTS AT HIGH LEVEL . . .

United States rice exports to foreign countries and shipments to domestic possessions combined for the 1939-40 marketing year August-July amounted to 653 million pounds (paddy included and converted to a milled-rice basis) as compared with 618 million pounds for the preceding year and 659 million pounds in 1937-38, which was the largest amount for any season since the post-World War years. Total exports and shipments during 1939-40 represented approximately 45 percent of the 1939 crop.

Exports to foreign countries in the 1939-40 season were about 20 million pounds below the preceding year, with the decline primarily due to the decreased takings by European countries. Exports to Europe during the last 6 months of the marketing year fell off very sharply, amounting to only 13 million pounds as compared with 29 million during the first half of the year. For the 3 months, May-July, exports to Europe showed an even greater decline, amounting to only a little over 1 million pounds as compared with 15 million pounds exported during the same 3 months of 1939. Increased exports during 1939-40 were made to Sweden, Switzerland, and Italy. Large shipments were made to Sweden and Switzerland during October and November as a result of the heavy purchases made shortly after the outbreak of the European War. Exports to Italy, normally the largest European rice-exporting country, amounted to 4,600,000 pounds and were shipped chiefly during the months of February to April.

RICE: United States exports to specified countries, August-July, average 1932-33 to 1936-37, annual 1937-38 to 1939-40 a/

Country	Average 1932-33 to 1936-37	1937-38	1938-39	1939-40
	1,000 pounds	1,000 pounds	1,000 pounds	1,000 pounds
Germany.............	11,493	1,449	180	0
United Kingdom.......	9,874	7,350	10,782	10,600
Belgium.............	7,049	15,211	13,349	4,561
France..............	13,164	8,507	78	541
Netherlands.........	4,362	11,641	9,464	1,564
Greece..............	5,639	16,180	12,580	3,243
Sweden..............	2,382	3,248	2,982	7,416
Denmark.............	645	0	4,168	1,823
Other Europe........	4,499	6,463	5,909	12,067
Total Europe........	59,107	70,049	59,492	41,815
Chile...............	3,784	21,806	3,760	1
Argentina...........	2,426	7,113	0	0
Venezuela...........	b/	b/	318	2,679
Canada..............	8,772	14,388	19,006	15,159
Central America.....	735	1,359	429	708
Cuba................	22,265	203,261	239,449	239,514
Other countries.....	1,606	7,793	3,668	6,634
Total non-Europe....	39,588	255,720	266,630	264,695
Total exports......	98,695	325,769	326,122	306,510

Compiled from official records, Bureau of Foreign and Domestic Commerce.
a/ Includes rough converted to clean rice.
b/ Included with "Other countries."

Cuba was again the outstanding export market for American rice, taking 78 percent of the exports as compared with 73 percent in the preceding year. It is of interest to note that exports to Cuba have been

at a high level during recent months. For the 6 months, February–July,
exports to Cuba amounted to 149 million pounds as compared with 90 million pounds during the first half of the marketing year. According to
unofficial figures from Habana, Cuban rice imports for the month of July
1940 amounted to 26 million pounds and were entirely from the United
States.

Rice shipments to domestic possessions for the 1939–40 marketing
year amounted to 346 million pounds as compared with the previous record
of 333 million pounds established in the 1937–38 season. The large increase for the 12-month period ended July 31 went to Puerto Rico. The
reasons given for the larger takings by this market during the past season were (1) an improved economic situation and (2) small stocks on hand
at the beginning of the season because of the reduced imports during the
1938–39 season.

RICE: United States shipments to possessions, August–July,
average 1932-33 to 1936-37, annual 1937-38 to 1939-40 a/

Country of destination	Average 1932-33 to 1936-37	1937-38	1938-39	1939-40
	1,000 pounds	1,000 pounds	1,000 pounds	1,000 pounds
Puerto Rico........	220,190	255,509	211,284	263,409
Hawaii............	81,331	75,972	78,531	81,159
Alaska............	1,079	1,204	1,102	971
Virgin Islands.....	b/	552	1,382	563
Total..........	302,600	333,237	292,299	346,102

Compiled from official records, Bureau of Foreign and Domestic Commerce.
a/ Includes rough converted to clean rice.
b/ Not reported prior to 1935.

- - - - - -

JAPANESE 1940 RICE CROP
PROSPECTS FAVORABLE . . .

Japanese rice production in 1940 is considered favorable, based
on recent information, according to a radiogram received from the United
States commercial attaché at Tokyo. Cold weather in late July was reported
to have delayed growth, but warm August weather has materially improved
crop prospects. No record crop is anticipated, but it is predicted that
the harvest will be larger than the average of the past 5 years, which
amounted to 593 million bushels.

Growing conditions for the Chosen rice crop are reported as
slightly unfavorable. Last year the Chosen crop was the smallest in 10
years, being estimated at 130 million bushels compared with 220 million
bushels in 1938. Fertilizer shortages in Japan and Chosen are reported

likely to reduce rice yields somewhat this season. During the 1939-40
season, Japan has had to import a substantial volume of foreign rice because of the very short supply available from Chosen.

      Official control over the distribution of rice was extended by
the recent ordinance of the Ministry of Agriculture and Forestry. Effective September 10, all rice must be distributed through the Government-
controlled distribution agencies, and even farmers residing in producing
areas will be required to obtain rice supplies from officially recognized
sales of commercial agencies. Regulations are also reported to provide
for a complete ban on the barter of rice in rural districts.

                            - - - - - -

BRAZILIAN RICE
EXPORTS DECLINE . . .

      Rice exports from Porto Alegre, Brazil, for the first 4 months
(April-July) of the new marketing year have declined nearly 50 percent as
compared with the same months in 1939, according to a report from the
American consulate at Porto Alegre. Exports for the 4 months this year
amounted to 177,000 bags 1/ as compared with 337,000 bags for the same
period last season. The greatest decline has occurred in shipments to
Europe, while exports to Argentina were also below a year ago. Increased
exports this season were made to Bolivia and to Canada.

      Shipments of rice from Porto Alegre to other parts of Brazil this
season are somewhat below last year. For the 4 months April to July
shipments this year amounted to 574,000 bags as compared with 757,000
bags for the same period in 1939.

      Despite a somewhat smaller Brazilian rice crop this year, rice
prices have been about the same as last year's low level for the Japanese
variety and slightly lower for Blue Rose. In July the price for Blue Rose,
the principal variety exported, averaged $1.74 per 100 pounds for "extra,"
milled in bags, at Porto Alegre as compared with $1.97 for July 1939.
Japanese "extra," milled in bags, in July averaged $1.56 per 100 pounds as
compared with $1.47 for the same month last year. The Rice Institute of
Rio Grande do Sul has endeavored to improve rice prices by purchases
through its regional agencies. By the end of July, the Institute had purchased 240,000 bags (of 110 pounds) of first-class unmilled of Japanese
and Blue Rose varieties. The report states that during July, purchases
by the Institute had little influence on prices either for export or in
the domestic market.

_____

1/ Shipments are reported in bags with no indication as to whether milled or
unmilled; a bag of milled rice weighs 132 pounds and unmilled 110 pounds.

- - - - - - -

V E G E T A B L E   O I L S   A N D   O I L S E E D S

UNITED STATES SOYBEAN-OIL EXPORTS
IN JULY ABOVE LAST YEAR . . . . . .

Soybean-oil exports from the United States during July were
above 1,000,000 pounds, as compared with 239,000 pounds in July 1939.
Shipments to Cuba and Chile showed an increase over the previous month;
however, Canada and Finland, consistent purchasers in recent months,
fell far below their monthly average for the current marketing year.
This loss was overcome, to some extent, by the 428,000 pounds of oil exported to the French West Indies. Oil exports for the 10 months this
season are equivalent to approximately 2 million bushels of beans.

Exports of soybeans for the month of July were only 106 bushels,
going to Cuba and Australia, while 788,301 bushels were exported in July
1939 to Denmark, France, Sweden, the United Kingdom and Australia. The
total for the months October-July amounted to 10,949,000 bushels, as
compared with 4,322,000 bushels for the same period in 1938-39.

UNITED STATES: Soybean-oil exports and imports,
July 1940, with comparisons

Item and country	July		October-July	
	1939	1940	1938-39	1939-40
	1,000 pounds.	1,000 pounds	1,000 pounds	1,000 pounds
Exports -				
Cuba....................	123	192	4,570	3,405
Switzerland.............	-	-	-	2,480
Finland.................	-	50	-	3,138
Sweden..................	-	-	-	1,076
Canada..................	-	61	14	1,801
Netherlands West Indies.......	21	31	466	667
Costa Rica..............	12	16	100	444
Iceland.................	-	34	-	326
Norway..................	-	-	2	211
Panama..................	3	10	19	327
Union of South Africa.........	29	7	241	149
Others..................	51	673	634	2,355
Total...............	239	1,074	6,046	16,379
Imports -	41	5	2,398	5,031

Compiled from official records, Bureau of Foreign and Domestic Commerce.

CHILE ESTABLISHES IMPORT QUOTA
FOR EDIBLE OILS . . . . . .

        In February 1939 the Chilean Government placed edible oils, under
an import-licensing system and established a quota of 2,200,000 pounds
of olive oil, 661,000 pounds of other edible oils for the Magallanes and
Aysen Zones, and 220,500 pounds for the remainder of the country. According to trade statistics, only 569,000 pounds of olive oil were imported
in 1939, due, no doubt, to the European situation; however, approximately
2,821,000 pounds of soybean oil were brought in during that period. Figures for other edible oils are not available at this time. Soybean-oil
exports from the United States to Chile during the first 7 months of 1940
amounted to 508,000 pounds, while none were recorded for the same months
in 1939.

        Decree No. 1012 of the Ministry for Foreign Affairs and Commerce,
published in the Diario Oficial of July 31, 1940, provided for the con-
tinuance of the import-licensing system and established the same quotas
as for the previous year with the stipulation that the Import License
Commission might increase these quotas by as much as 50 percent if they
deemed such a measure necessary.

        Import licenses must be authorized by the Commission of Interna-
tional Exchange. This decree became effective on July 31, 1940, and re-
mains in force until May 31, 1941.

                        - - - - - - -

EXPERIMENTS IN REFINED AVOCADO OIL
SUCCESSFUL IN GUATEMALA . . . . . .

        Experiments in the manufacture of refined avocado oil are being
made in Guatemala and may replace olive oil in that market, according to
a report from American Vice Consul Kathleen Molesworth at Guatemala.
Arrangements have been made to produce this oil on a commercial scale.

        Avocados are grown in all parts of Guatemala, but there is very
little actual cultivation of the tree, and no large plantations exist.
The avocado is widely used as a food, and this demand maintains the price
at a fairly high level, so that there are seldom large surplus stocks
available at low prices. With no concentration of production, the manu-
facturers of oil are faced with the problem of collecting the avocados
from a number of small producers and it is possible that at times this
will retard production of oil. The refined oil is light in color, much
like olive oil, and is said to be free from taste or odor and high in
vitamin content, which should prove beneficial as an item of diet.

                    * * * * * * *

- - - - - -

C O T T O N - O T H E R   F I B E R S

LIVERPOOL COTTON MARKET
SHOWS LITTLE CHANGE . . .

Spinner demand in the Liverpool spot market was well maintained
during the week ended August 30, according to a cable received from the
American Embassy at London. Interest centered around better staples,
while for other qualities inquiry was fair to moderate. The week's sales
aggregated about 40,000 bales. Due to the small (unchanged) September
shipping quota for American cotton, demand for spot lots of American at
Liverpool showed some increase during the week. A relatively large business was reported in Belgian Congo cotton, and it was rumored that the
Cotton Controller has agreed to free imports from the Congo on a sterling
payment basis. Indian growths are reported to have met with fair demand.

C.i.f. import buying of American cotton has exhausted the commercial
shipping quota for September, so that little further business seems possible until the October quota is announced. Business in Brazilian and
Peruvian c.i.f. cottons continued to be paralyzed as a result of a lack of
license allotments for purchases made after May 30. There was rather more
business in Indian and African due to improvement in the freight supply.

Manchester reported somewhat larger inquiry for cloth exports
during the week, but actual business remained difficult, partly on ac-
count of keen Japanese and American competition in some important markets.
Lancashire cotton-mill activity was unchanged compared with a week earlier.

- - - - - - -

SOUTHERN BRAZIL'S COTTON CROP
MOVING SLOWLY . . . . . .

Exports of cotton from Brazil during the first 5 months (April-
August) of the Southern Brazil cotton season amounted to less than 500,000
bales compared with 1,052,000 bales in the corresponding period of 1939,
according to recent reports received from Sao Paulo. Shipments to
Japan since April were estimated at about 190,000 bales, while exports to
the United Kingdom totaled about 120,000 bales. The extension of the
British naval blockade to include the Mediterranean area and all western
Europe, except normal shipments to Spain and Portugal, seriously retarded
the movement of Southern Brazil's new-crop cotton, which had just begun
to reach the markets abroad.

Exports of Brazilian cotton to Japan have been hindered for some
time by a shortage of freight space, although the overbought position of
Japanese importers tends to restrict new purchases to some extent. British purchases of the new Brazilian crop have not been as high as last

year, due largely to difficulty in obtaining import licenses and allotments of shipping space from the British Government. Shipments to Canada have increased considerably over last year's figure although still an insignificant part of total cotton exports from Brazil. Carry-over is expected to be much larger than usual unless conditions in Europe and the Orient improve in the next few months.

Prices of Brazilian cotton have declined in recent months to such an extent as to give it a decided advantage over comparable grades of American. Reports received from Japan indicate that this price spread, as quoted on the cotton exchange at Osaka, averaged between 2 and 3 cents per pound during July. Exports of Brazilian cotton to China were also reported to be increasing as a result of relatively lower prices when compared with other growths of similar grade. The 1939-40 cotton crop for all Brazil, estimated at 1,982,000 bales, was only slightly less than the 1,989,000-bale crop of 1938-39 and the record crop of 2,078,000 bales produced in 1937-38. Consequently, the supply available for export during the current season should be roughly equivalent to the average annual exports in recent years, of about 1.3 million bales.

- - - - - - -

CANADIAN COTTON MILLS REDUCE
ACTIVITY IN LAST HALF OF 1940 . . .

Cotton-textile mills in Canada entered a period of reduced activity in the latter half of June, following about 9 months of heavy production for wartime demand, according to a report from American Consul Joseph I. Touchette at Montreal. Mill consumption of raw cotton since the outbreak of war has been about 75 percent above that of the corresponding period of 1938-39. The increase was attributed to advance buying for domestic distribution as well as to large orders from the British and Canadian Governments for war-material supplies. Total mill consumption in Canada during the first 6 months of 1940 was placed at 193,000 bales compared with 104,000 bales and 111,000 bales in the corresponding periods of 1939 and 1938, respectively. United States exports of raw cotton to Canada during 1939-40 (August-July) amounted to 432,000 bales compared with 238,000 bale in 1938-39 and 262,000 bales in 1937-38.

Imports of cotton piecegoods from the United States during the 9 months under review were triple those of a year ago. Important increases were also registered in imports from Japan, while British-made goods maintained the pre-war import level. It was reported that consumption has not equaled the total of imports and production so that large stocks of cotton goods have accumulated in the hands of distributors, retarding the current volume of new business. Mills producing for the domestic market are rapidly completing their backlog orders and are again seeking new business.

The recent high rate of civilian consumption of cotton goods has showed signs of diminishing, as considerable increases were noted in prices of cotton goods (12 to 17 percent higher than in September 1939). Increases in taxation and the general cost of living also were factors detracting from consumer-purchasing power. Canadian mills report that the keen competition previously offered by American-made goods is expected to be somewhat restricted by the recently imposed War Exchange Tax of 10 percent.

- - - - - - -

EARLY MONTHS OF PAST SEASON
FAVORABLE TO AMERICAN COTTON EXPORTS . . .

Shipments of cotton from the United States increased to 6.4 million bales (of 500 pounds gross) in the 11 months, August-June 1939-40, from 3.4 million in the same months of the 1938-39 season. While this increase is very considerable, shipments in 1939-40 remained below the 10-year average, 1923-24 to 1932-33. With the exception of Central Europe, all the larger European countries increased their purchases of American cotton in the early part of the 1939-40 season, and prior to the intensification of warfare in the spring of 1940, imports ran high. The United Kingdom, leading as a purchaser, took 44 percent of the total exports to European markets during the 1939-40 season.

The extraordinary increase in exports to Europe in 1939-40 has been largely due to special factors. Exports in 1938-39 had been particularly small, stocks as a result had been depleted, and higher imports in 1939-40 appeared necessary to make good the previous year's deficiency. Moreover, for some time, the outbreak of war increased mill requirements and made it desirable to lay in emergency stocks as well. Recent war developments and the consequent extension of the British blockade have meanwhile virtually cut off United States cotton shipments to the European continent, except for exports to Spain and Portugal. Shipments to Japan, although 2 percent above last season's level, were far below the 10-year average. Purchases by Canada, however, were not only above last season's level but were more than double those of the average of 1923-24 to 1932-33. Shipments to China and British India were also above the 1938-39 level and the 10-year average.

From August to June 1939-40, shipments of cotton from Egypt, though slightly less than in the preceding season, were 17 percent above the 10-year average. Of the total cotton exported, the United Kingdom took 626,000 bales (of 478 pounds net) or 39 percent, compared with 527,000 bales a year earlier. France, ranking second as a purchaser of the Egyptian fiber, took 19 percent of the total exports during the 1939-40 season, compared with 11 percent a year earlier. Both the United States and British India also increased their purchases.

Cotton exports from Brazil from August to June, 1939-40, were 33 percent below the high level reached in the corresponding months of 1938-39.

Increased shipments to the United Kingdom, Portugal, and the Netherlands
failed to offset the loss in exports to Japan, Germany, and other countries.

During the 11 months, August-June 1939-40, total exports of cotton
from Peru were 3 percent below the corresponding 11 months a year earlier.
Shipments to the United Kingdom, the leading market, were the highest on
record and represented 61 percent of total exports. The loss of Germany
as a market for Peruvian cotton was partially offset by increased shipments
to the United Kingdom, Japan, and Italy.

Exports of cotton from Argentina during August-June 1939-40
increased 5 percent over the same period of 1938-39, and were 32 percent
above the 6-year average, 1924-25 to 1929-30. Of the total number of bales
exported during the current season, the United Kingdom took 35 percent,
Italy 24 percent, and Germany 17 percent.

The Sudan, during August-June 1939-40, exported less than one-half
as much cotton as was exported a year earlier. The United Kingdom, the
leading market prior to 1939-40, took only 33 percent of the total exports,
compared with 61 percent a year ago. British India now taking first place,
purchased 35 percent of the total exports, compared with only 15 percent
last season.

Data for exports of cotton from British India are available only
through April 1940.

COTTON: Summary of world exports, August-June, average 1923-24
          to 1932-33, and seasons, 1936-37 to 1939-40

| Exporting countries | August-June | | | | |
| | Quantity | | | | |
	Average 1923-24 to 1932-33	1936-37	1937-38	1938-39	1939-40
	1,000 bales	1,000 bales	1,000 bales	1,000 bales	1,000 bales
United States................	7,876	5,560	5,771	3,399	6,379
British India................	2,570	3,375	1,548	2,404	a/
Egypt........................	1,381	1,768	1,667	1,640	1,622
Brazil.......................	83	921	970	1,291	872
Peru.........................	174	305	256	300	290
Argentina....................	72	139	24	86	90
Sudan........................	96	244	235	291	135
Total 7 countries...........	12,252	12,312	10,471	9,411	-
Total excluding British India	9,682	8,937	8,923	7,007	9,388

Compiled from official sources.
a/ Data not available since April. August-April figures were 1,401,000
bales compared with 1,774,000 bales a year earlier.

COTTON: Exports from principal exporting countries, August–June, average 1923-24 to 1932-33, and seasons 1937-38 to 1939-40[a]/

Destination of exports from principal exporting countries	August–June							
	Quantity				Percentage of total			
	Average 1923-24 to 1932-33	1937-38	1938-39	1939-40	Average 1923-24 to 1932-33	1937-38	1938-39	1939-40
Exports from the United States to	1,000 bales	1,000 bales	1,000 bales	1,000 bales	Percent	Percent	Percent	Percent
Germany *	1,803	694	330	20	23	12	10	b/
United Kingdom	1,743	1,619	413	1,946	22	28	12	30
France	846	767	359	768	11	13	11	12
Italy	677	516	276	577	9	9	8	9
Spain	290	1	17	295	4	b/	1	5
Belgium	189	199	92	215	2	3	3	3
Soviet Union	c/ 174	d/	0	0	2	b/	0	0
Netherlands	136	124	71	172	2	2	2	3
Sweden	58	88	96	207	1	2	3	3
Portugal	44	40	11	35	1	1	b/	1
Poland and Danzig	24	241	168	5	b/	4	5	b/
Other Europe	63	278	295	204	b/	5	8	4
Total Europe	6,047	4,567	2,128	4,444	77	79	63	70
Canada	200	248	223	411	2	4	7	6
Japan	1,254	648	877	898	16	11	26	14
China	277	23	85	419	4	b/	3	7
British India	81	148	3	90	1	3	b/	1
Other countries	17	137	83	127	b/	3	1	2
Total	7,876	5,771	3,399	6,389	100	100	100	100
Egypt								
United Kingdom	542	543	527	626	39	33	32	39
France	180	224	182	314	13	13	11	19
United States	159	35	36	57	12	2	2	4
Germany e/	100	207	204	12	7	12	12	1
Italy	93	110	102	97	7	7	6	6
Japan	62	79	146	140	4	5	9	9
Switzerland	60	74	73	68	4	4	4	4
Spain	45	1	16	10	3	b/	1	1
Czechoslovakia	29	57	43	1	2	3	3	b/
British India	24	127	80	116	2	8	5	7
Belgium-Luxemburg	16	17	18	f/ 14	1	1	1	1
Poland and Danzig	12	41	42	3	1	2	3	b/
Other countries	59	152	171	164	5	10	11	9
Total	1,381	1,667	1,640	1,622	100	100	100	100

*Includes shipments through the free port of Bremen, much of which is afterward shipped to other countries.

Continued –

COTTON: Exports from principal exporting countries, August-June,
average 1923-24 to 1932-33, and seasons 1937-38 to 1939-40-Con.

Destination of exports from principal exporting countries	August-June							
	Quantity				Percentage of total			
	Average 1923-24 to 1932-33	1937-38	1938-39	1939-40	Average 1923-24 to 1932-33	1937-38	1938-39	1939-
	1,000 bales	1,000 bales	1,000 bales	1,000 bales	Percent	Percent	Percent	Percer
Exports from Brazil to								
United Kingdom..	–	184	201	273	–	19	16	31
Japan............	–	144	359	179	–	15	28	21
China..........	–	10	153	f/109	–	1	12	13
Germany........	–	459	252	70	–	47	19	8
France........	–	57	133	56	–	6	10	6
Portugal.......	–	28	9	f/ 41	–	3	1	5
Netherlands.....	–	16	37	38	–	2	3	4
Italy..........	–	11	59	27	–	1	5	3
Belgium-Luxem. .	–	26	26	22	–	3	2	3
Spain..........	–	0	9	f/ 3	–	0	1	b/
United States...	–	d/	3	f/ 2	–	b/	b/	b/
Poland..........	–	22	26	f/ 1	–	2	2	b/
Other countries.	–	13	24	51	–	1	1	5
Total........	g/83	970	1,291	872	100	100	100	100
Peru to								
United Kingdom..	–	139	149	177	–	54	50	61
Japan...........	–	5	16	27	–	2	5	9
Netherlands.....	–	6	22	19	–	2	7	7
Italy..........	–	3	2	14	–	1	1	5
Chile..........	–	9	8	10	–	4	3	4
France.........	–	8	9	9	–	3	3	3
Belgium........	–	10	15	9	–	4	5	3
Germany........	–	73	74	7	–	28	25	2
United States...	–	d/	d/	6	–	b/	b/	2
China..........	–	d/	1	3	–	b/	b/	1
Other countries.	–	3	4	9	–	2	1	3
Total.........	g/174	256	300	290	100	100	100	100
Argentina to								
United Kingdom..	h/ 32	d/	2	31	47	1	2	35
Germany........	h/ 10	19	65	15	14	80	75	17
France.........	h/ 7	0	0	0	10	0	0	0
Spain..........	h/ 7	0	0	0	10	0	0	0
Belgium........	h/ 5	d/	d/	1	7	b/	b/	1
Italy.........	h/ 4	d/	d/	21	7	b/	1	24
Chian.........	h/ i/	i/		5	–	–	–	5
Other countries.	h/ 3	5	19	17	5	19	22	18
Total.........	h/ 68	24	86	90	100	100	100	100

Continued-

COTTON: Exports from principal exporting countries, August–June, average 1923–24 to 1932–33, and seasons 1937–38 to 1939–40 – Continued

Destination of exports from principal exporting countries	August–June							
	Quantity				Percentage of total			
	Average 1923–24 to 1932–33	1937–38	1938–39	1939–40	Average 1923–24 to 1932–33	1937–38	1938–39	1939–40
Exports from Sudan to	1,000 bales	1,000 bales	1,000 bales	1,000 bales	Percent	Percent	Percent	Percent
United Kingdom..	92	125	178	44	96	53	61	33
British India...	i/	68	43	48	–	29	15	35
France..........	2	14	21	24	3	6	7	18
Italy...........	d/	8	10	9	b/	3	4	6
Switzerland.....	i/	3	7	4	–	1	2	3
United States...	i/	3	8	1	–	1	3	1
Japan...........	i/	1	12	d/	–	b/	4	b/
Poland..........	i/	5	3	d/	–	2	1	b/
Germany.........	c/	4	1	0	b/	2	b/	0
Netherlands.....	i/	3	1	0	–	1	b/	0
Other countries.	2	1	7	5	1	2	3	4
Total..........	96	235	291	135	100	100	100	100

Compiled from official sources. a/ Bales of 478 pounds net except for the United States and Peru which are 500 pounds gross. b/ Less than 0.5 percent. c/ Excludes Russia in Asia. d/ Less than 500 bales. e/ Beginning January 1, 1938, includes Austria. f/ Ten months, August–May. g/ Data not available by countries. h/ Six-year average, 1924–25 to 1929–30. i/ If any, included in "Other countries."

BOMBAY COTTON PRICES REACT UNFAVORABLY
TO RECENT WAR DEVELOPMENTS . . . . . .

        The sharp decline of cotton prices at Bombay during May as a result of the German invasion of France, Belgium, and the Netherlands was continued through-out June, after Italy's entry into the war, according to a report from American Vice Consul Daniel V. Anderson at Bombay. The July–August Broach contract quoted on April 30, 1940, at a price equivalent to 10.33 cents per pound had declined to 7.42 cents on June 1 and 5.90 cents on June 29. Prices for July and August have risen somewhat above the low level for June.

        The closing of the Mediterranean route following the entry of Italy into the war not only excluded Indian cotton from the markets of continental Europe but greatly increased the shipping cost as well as the time required for delivery of British purchases. The unsettled political situation in the Orient and diffi-culties experienced by Japanese importers in securing foreign-exchange permits had a disturbing effect on the Bombay market.

COTTON STATISTICS . . .

COTTON: Spot prices per pound of representative raw cotton at Liverpool, August 30, 1940, with comparisons

Description	1940						
	July		August				
	19	26	2	9	16	23	30
	Cents	Cents	Cents	Cents	Cents	Cents	Cents
American –							
Middling...................	13.15	13.33	13.11	13.15	13.74	13.72	13.80
Low Middling..............	12.46	12.75	12.61	12.65	13.23	13.22	13.30
Egyptian (Fully Good Fair) –							
Giza 7..................	18.11	18.67	19.49	20.46	21.85	21.53	22.42
Uppers...................	19.10	19.37	19.34	20.14	21.01	20.71	21.32
Brazilian (Fair) –							
North....................	12.04	12.33	12.19	12.23	12.31	12.30	12.96
Sao Paulo................	12.54	12.83	12.70	12.73	13.32	13.30	13.47
Indian –							
Broach (Fully Good) –	10.35	10.52	10.43	10.26	10.35	10.23	10.30
Central Provinces (Superfine)–	10.31	12.08	12.08	12.16	12.58	12.46	12.53
Oomra No. 1 (Fine) –	9.44	9.61	9.53	9.61	9.95	9.83	9.89
Sind (Fine) –	10.52	–	–	–	–	–	–

Compiled from the Weekly Circular of the Liverpool Cotton Association, Ltd. and the New York Cotton Exchange Daily Report. Quotations converted from sterling at official rates.

– – – – – –

UNITED STATES: Exports of cotton to principal foreign markets, annual 1938-39 and 1939-40, and August 1 to 31, 1939 and 1940 a/
(Running bales)

Country to which exported	Year ended July 31		August 1 to 31	
	1938-39	1939-40	1939	1940
	1,000 bales	1,000 bales	1,000 bales	1,000 bales
United Kingdom............	478	2,019	96	32
Continental Europe........	1,792	2,478	133	0
Total Europe............	2,270	4,497	229	32
Japan.....................	905	960	36	5
Other countries...........	393	990	23	16
Total.................	3,568	6,447	238	53
Linters...................	215	0	33	2
Total, excluding linters.	3,353	6,447	255	51

Compiled from Weekly Stock and Movement Report, New York Cotton Exchange. a/ Includes linters.

T O B A C C O

CANADIAN TOBACCO CROP GREATLY REDUCED
BUT TOTAL SUPPLIES REMAIN LARGE . . .

An unusually early frost on the night of August 23 in Norfolk
County, Ontario, where most of Canada's flue-cured tobacco is grown, destroyed about 10,000 acres of the crop. The area left for harvest in all
of Canada is now expected to produce only about 37.2 million pounds as
compared with the record 1939 flue-cured crop of 82.6 million pounds, according to an official report released by the Dominion Bureau of Statistics.

The acreage of types other than flue-cured, for which no frost
damage is reported, is substantially below that of 1939, and the combined
production of all types is expected to be only about half as large as the
record 1939 crop of 109.8 million pounds. On the other hand, stocks of
old Canadian leaf at the end of June 1940 (including approximately 6.0
million pounds of flue-cured from the 1939 crop still in the hands of farmers) were exceptionally large, totaling approximately 118.0 million pounds
as compared with only 86.1 million on June 30, 1939, and 67.8 million
pounds in 1938. Most of the increase in stocks results from the exceptionally large flue-cured crop in 1939 and curtailed exports to the United
Kingdom.

The large current carry-over combined with the short 1940 production
indicates a total supply materially below that of a year ago but well above
that of previous years. The short 1940 crop will therefore not necessarily
result in larger imports of American leaf, but will limit export supplies.
It will also enable the sale of flue-cured leaf from the 1939 crop still
held by farmers.

CANADA: Acreage, yield, and production of flue-cured tobacco,
1938-1940

Province and year	Acreage	Yield	Pro- duction	Province and year	Acreage	Yield	Pro- duction
			1,000				1,000
	Acres	Pounds	pounds	British	Acres	Pounds	pounds
Ontario -				Columbia -			
1938.....	61,300	1,244	76,279	1938......	380.	1,039	395
1939.....	62,550	1,250	78,185	1939......	310	1,032	320
1940 a/..	b/32,353	1,000	32,353	1940 a/...	400	1,000	400
Quebec -				All Canada-			
1938.....	1,850	811	1,500	1938......	63,530	1,231	78,174
1939.....	5,710	722	4,120	1939......	68,570	1,205	82,625
1940 a/..	5,520	800	4,416	1940 a/...	b/38,273	971	37,169

Compiled from reports of the Dominion Bureau of Statistics, Ottawa.
a/ Preliminary. b/ Excludes 10,000 acres estimated as destroyed by frost.

EXPORTS OF CUBAN LEAF MAINTAINED
BUT CIGAR EXPORTS DOWN . . . . . .

Exports of leaf tobacco from Cuba during the past several months
have increased slightly in spite of unsettled world conditions, but cigar
exports have declined sharply, according to a report of American Consul
Cyril L. F. Thiel at Habana. Leaf and cigar exports to the United States
have increased, leaf shipments to Europe have been maintained, but cigar
exports to that area have been greatly curtailed.

Leaf exports during 1939, which were slightly above the average
of recent years, totaled 28.8 million pounds as compared with 28.0 million
in 1938, and shipments during the first 7 months (January-July) of 1940
totaled 18.0 million as compared with 16.4 million pounds in the corresponding months of the previous year. The increase in exports in 1939
resulted from larger shipments to the United States, which totaled 15.0
million pounds as compared with 13.1 million in 1938.

The increase during the first 7 months of 1940 resulted primarily
from larger shipments to Spain, which were more than double those of the
corresponding months in 1939. Exports to the Netherlands, Sweden, and
France, which were made early in the year, were somewhat larger, and
shipments to Argentina, Uruguay, and Canada were substantially higher
than during the first 7 months in 1940. Exports to the United States were
only slightly above those of the corresponding period in 1939 and totaled
8.9 million pounds as compared with 8.7 million for the preceding year.
The rate of export in 1940 was well within the United States quota rate,
which provides for the yearly entry into this country of 22 million pounds
of cigar filler and scrap tobacco at a duty rate on an unstemmed basis of
17.5 cents per pound or one-half the full duty.

CUBA: Exports of leaf tobacco, by countries, 1935 to 1939,
and January-July 1940 a/

Year	United States	Germany	Nether-lands	Spain	Argen-tina	Others	Total
	1,000 pounds	1,000 pounds	1,000 pounds	1,000 pounds	1,000 pounds	1,000 pounds	1,000 pounds
1935......	15,825	3,960	551	6,627	1,229	3,147	31,339
1936......	11,595	3,231	558	3,510	777	3,378	23,049
1937......	13,791	4,956	1,244	2,932	994	3,462	27,379
1938......	13,141	3,496	920	6,605	1,270	2,596	28,028
1939 b/...	14,963	1,863	2,180	6,446	947	2,387	28,786
Jan.-July. 1940 b/	8,889	c/	c/	c/	c/	9,153	18,042

Compiled from Comercio Exterior República de Cuba.
a/ Includes strips and scrap.
b/ Preliminary.
c/ Not separately reported, included with "Others."

Exports of Cuban cigars have decreased sharply in the past 19
months. Exports during 1939, as a result of smaller shipments to Europe,
totaled 29.5 million pieces as compared with 32.6 million in 1938. Exports during the first 7 months of 1940 decreased more drastically and
totaled only 7.7 million pieces as compared with 18.4 million during the
corresponding period in 1939. The decrease in 1940 resulted largely from
an embargo by the United Kingdom, which practically eliminated cigar imports into that country. In recent years the United Kingdom has taken
about half of Cuba's cigar export.

CUBA: Exports of cigars, by countries, 1935 to 1939,
and January-July 1940

Year	United States	United Kingdom	Spain	France	Germany	Others	Total
	1,000 pieces	1,000 pieces	1,000 pieces	1,000 pieces	1,000 pieces	1,000 pieces	1,000 pieces
1935......	3,830	21,035	9,820	1,898	334	4,023	40,940
1936......	2,960	23,258	8,513	1,879	526	4,858	42,054
1937......	3,096	21,077	1,875	3,440	565	5,709	35,762
1938......	2,457	17,520	4,028	2,807	413	5,409	32,634
1939 a/ ..	3,195	16,560	2,582	b/	b/	7,154	29,491
Jan.-July 1940 a/	1,460	b/	b/	b/	b/	6,262	7,722

Compiled from Comercio Exterior República de Cuba.
a/Preliminary. b/Not separately reported, included with "others."

- - - - - - -

THAILAND INCREASES LEAF PRODUCTION AND
CUTS IMPORTS OF AMERICAN 60 PERCENT . . .

Fiscal and control measures imposed early in 1939 by the Thailand
(Siam) Government, and depreciation in value of the Nation's currency
which has occurred since the beginning of the European War have reduced
the country's imports of tobacco, largely of American origin, and have
resulted in the domestic production of flue-cured leaf being expanded.
Imports of leaf and cigarettes for the fiscal year 1939-40 were in each
case about 60 percent below those of the preceding year, and the acreage
of flue-cured tobacco for harvest in 1940 is more than double that of previous years, according to American Vice Consul Harlan B. Clark at Bangkok.

Imports of leaf into Thailand from the United States, almost entirely
flue-cured, dropped from 3.3 million pounds for the year April-March 1938-39
to 1.6 million pounds in 1939-40. Imports of cigarettes (which are made
largely from American flue-cured leaf) from the United Kingdom and other
sources, dropped from 2.3 million pounds to 0.9 million pounds. The domestic manufacture of cigarettes was also curtailed but not as drastically as

imports. Decreased supplies of foreign leaf for use in manufacture were
offset in part by greater utilization of domestic flue-cured.

In order to prevent cigarette prices from being greatly increased
as a result of increased duty, the excise tax, and decrease in exchange
value of currency (from about 45 United States cents per thailand baht to
37 cents per baht), the Thailand Government on December 39, 1939, ordered
that cigarette prices could not be increased more than 10 percent over the
prices prevailing prior to December 1, 1939. This restriction tends to further encourage the substitution of cheap domestic leaf in place of American.

The country's production of flue-cured leaf, which was begun only a
few years ago, has been greatly increased. The acreage of the crop for
harvest in 1940 is estimated at about 4,000 acres, which is believed to be
more than double the 1939 acreage and more than four times that of 1938.
The Government is taking an active part in encouraging production expansion
in order to curtail imports, but the provisions of the tobacco act of March
1939, which provided for Government monopoly over the purchase of leaf from
farmers, has not been put into force. A large foreign cigarette manufac-
turing concern continues to be the principal buyer of the crop. The Govern-
ment-owned cigarette factory, which was purchased from a private agency in
May 1939, is being expanded, additional machines added, and is expected to
begin operation at an early date. Three privately owned factories in Bangkok have continued to operate.

THAILAND: Imports of leaf tobacco and cigarettes,
1934-35 to 1939-40

Year beginning April 1	United States	United Kingdom	Singapore and Penang a/	Others b/	Total
	1,000 pounds	1,000 pounds	1,000 pounds	1,000 pounds	1,000 pounds
Leaf tobacco:					
1934...........	645	10	10	593	1,258
1935...........	1,169	7	90	363	1,629
1936...........	3,252	23	291	503	4,069
1937...........	3,507	159	1,439	384	5,489
1938...........	3,329	4	849	5	4,187
1939 c/........	1,570	d/	d/	77	1,647
Cigarettes:					
1934...........	3	4,029	314	270	4,616
1935...........	5	4,199	288	147	4,639
1936...........	d/	3,150	261	133	3,544
1937...........	1	2,813	281	53	3,148
1938...........	3	1,999	240	17	2,259
1939 c/........	4	862	51	18	935

Compiled from Thailand customs returns. a/ Includes Malay States.
b/ Largely China and Hong Kong. c/ Preliminary. d/ Less than 500 pounds.

* * * * * * *

- - - - - - -

F R U I T S, V E G E T A B L E S, A N D N U T S

UNITED STATES DRIED-APPLE EXPORTS
HALVED BY THE WAR. . . . .

    Exports of dried apples from the United States during the 1939-40 season, July to June, amounted to 8,370 short tons, or only about 52 percent of the movement during the previous season and of the average for the 5-years, 1931-32 to 1935-36. Exports to Europe totaled 7,653 tons, or about half the movement during 1938-39, while shipments to countries outside of Europe increased slightly. The Netherlands was the most important market, accounting for 39 percent of the total, followed by Sweden and the United Kingdom, with 18 percent each. Since March, exports to the Netherlands and other European markets have been negligible.

    UNITED STATES: Exports of dried apples, by countries, July-June, average 1931-32 to 1935-36, annual 1936-37 to 1939-40

Country	Average 1931-32 to 1935-36	1936-37	1937-38	1938-39	1939-40
	Short tons	Short tons	Short tons	Short tons	Short tons
Germany...................	6,594	799	781	1,053	10
Netherlands...............	3,726	2,677	4,655	5,948	3,294
United Kingdom............	854	518	1,140	1,170	1,519
France...................	1,612	3,762	2,140	2,630	218
Sweden...................	1,594	1,189	1,364	1,907	1,543
Belgium..................	206	432	382	667	34
Other Europe.............	1,201	685	1,162	1,796	1,035
Total Europe...........	15,787	10,062	11,624	15,171	7,653
Canada...................	49	134	34	59	47
Newfoundland and Labrador..	7	6	50	47	64
Netherlands Indies........	62	48	77	62	89
Palestine................	95	213	139	200	148
Others..................	28	176	294	276	369
Total ex-Europe.........	241	577	594	644	717
Total all countries....	16,128	10,639	12,218	15,815	8,370

Compiled from official sources.

- - - - - - -

WAR SERIOUSLY AFFECTING
BRITISH HONDURAS GRAPEFRUIT INDUSTRY . . .

    A serious crisis has been precipitated by the war in the British Honduras grapefruit industry, according to a report from American Vice Consul Culver E. Gidden At Belize. Production and exports have been expanding since the early 1930's with Government encouragement, but the

- - - - - - -

loss of the export market because of the war and the absence of a domestic
market have left large surpluses of fruit in the hands of growers.

Grapefruit is the most important citrus fruit produced in British
Honduras. Native seedling grapefruit are found throughout the country,
and the fruit is consumed domestically. Plantings probably total around
100 acres, and the trees, for the most part, average about 20 years old.

Grapefruit for export is produced on grafted, rather than seedling,
trees. Sour-orange root stock, which is best suited to the country, pre-
dominates, although some seedling Duncan, seedling native and shaddock, and
rough lemon are used. Until recently, large supplies of budded trees were
available, but plantings have fallen off and many nurseries abandoned because of low returns on the fruit and high transportation costs to export
markets.

About 1,000 acres of improved varieties of grapefruit are planted
in the Stann Creek Valley, 100 acres in the Corozal district, and 100 acres
scattered throughout the rest of the country. Of this, about one-third is
in full production, one-third coming into production and the balance of
nonbearing age.

Production in 1939-40 totaled 125,000 cases, of which 75 percent
was Marsh Seedless and the rest Duncans, a seeded variety. Fully 90 percent of last year's exports were Marsh Seedless. Within 5 years, export
production should reach 250,000 cases. No estimate is available on the
volume of citrus fruit sold locally.

Oranges, lemons, and limes are grown chiefly for domestic consumpti
About 145 acres of oranges are planted in the country, of which 20 acres
consist of Valencias; lemons total around 10 acres; and West Indies limes,
which are scattered throughout the country, about 2 acres.

BRITISH HONDURAS: Exports of grapefruit, by principal countries,
annual 1935-1939, January-June 1940

Country	1935	1936	1937	1938	1939	1940 a/
	1,000 boxes	1,000 boxes	1,000 boxes	1,000 boxes	1,000 boxes	1,000 boxes
United Kingdom.........	17	19	11	46	58	14
Canada.................	7	9	12	17	12	10
Others.................	1	2	1	2	1	0
Total...............	25	30	24	65	71	24

American consulate, Belize. Converted to boxes of 70 pounds.
a/ January-June.

British Honduras, slightly larger in size than the State of
Massachusetts, has only 58,000 people, the majority with very low purchasing power. Most of the inhabitants prefer the sweetness of an orange

to the tang of a grapefruit. Consequently, the home demand for grapefruit is limited, and the industry depends chiefly on the export market.

In the past, the United Kingdom and Canada have absorbed the bulk of exports from British Honduras. Exports to the United Kingdom rose sharply in 1938 and 1939. With the outbreak of war, however, shipments to the United Kingdom were severely curtailed. As a result, planters have looked to Canada for a market, despite the low prices prevailing in that country. Grapefruit exports are transshipped at Kingston, Jamaica.

Canning facilities were expanded in British Honduras during the past few years, but production has been practically discontinued since the signing of the Anglo-American trade agreement in January 1939, which placed American canned citrus products on the free list in the United Kingdom. Canned-fruit prices have advanced in the United Kingdom since the outbreak of war, but British Honduras exports have not benefited because of the lack of shipping facilities.

During the past decade, the British Honduras Government has encouraged the planting of grapefruit, but that policy has been reversed because of the competition of American and Palestinian fruit in export markets.

Conditions in the British Honduras fruit industry are not expected to improve until after the end of the war. A number of small planters have already abandoned their orchards. The principal wartime problem is that of securing transportation facilities, since shipping space has been reserved for more essential products. Consequently, growers have not benefited from the reduced competition in the United Kingdom of United States and Jaffa fruit.

- - - - - - - -

FREIGHT REDUCED ON
BRAZILIAN CITRUS . . .

The President of Brazil has approved the recommendations of the National Economic Defense Committee to reduce the freight rates on oranges, according to a report from American Commercial Attaché Walter J. Donnelly at Rio de Janeiro.

Approval has also been given to plans for establishing a cold-storage plant at the port of Rio de Janeiro. These measures are designed to assist the Brazilian citrus industry, which has been hard hit by the sharp curtailment of European purchases as a result of the war.

CANADIAN FRUIT AND VEGETABLE
DUTY VALUATION . . . . . .

     As a means of protecting domestic producers of fruits and vegetables
during their marketing season, the Canadian Government administers a system of advanced valuations over invoice values. The resulting higher valuations are the bases upon which regular and special seasonal duties are
calculated. These advanced valuations vary from year to year as to effective date, duration, and region, depending upon when local produce is on
the market. In order to keep American producers and distributors cur-
rently informed of the status of advanced valuations on the many fruits and
vegetables that are shipped to Canada, a calendar similar to the one below
will appear in future issues of Foreign Crops and Markets, noting the
action taken by the Canadian Government.

CANADA: Record of seasonal advanced valuation for calculating duty
on imports of fruits and vegetables, 1940-41

Commodity	Advanced valuation	Date estab- lished	Date Canceled	Region affected
	Cents per pound			
Prunes	1.0	Aug. 8		Western Canada
Plums	1.0	July 16		Western Canada
		Aug. 1		Ontario-Quebec
		Aug. 13		Maritime Provinces
Carrots	0.8	June 8	July 20	Ontario-Quebec
		June 15	July 29	Western Canada
		Aug. 13		Maritime Provinces
Cauliflower......	1.5	June 15		Western Canada
		Aug. 13		Maritime Provinces
Cantaloupes......	1.25	July 18		Western Canada
		July 24		Ontario-Quebec
		Aug. 13		Maritime Provinces
Pears	1.0	July 26		Western Canada
		Aug. 20		Ontario-Quebec
Cabbage..........	0.8	June 12	Aug. 20	Western Canada
		June 20		Maritime Provinces
Green peas........	2.0	June 8	Aug. 21	Ontario-Quebec
		June 11		Western Canada
		July 25		Maritime Provinces

Reports from Assistant Commercial Attache Oliver B. North at Ottawa.
Western Canada includes the Provinces of British Columbia, Alberta,
Saskatchewan, and Manitoba. The Maritime Provinces include Nova Scotia,
New Brunswick, and Prince Edwards Island.

G E N E R A L   A N D   M I S C E L L A N E O U S

GERMANY ADOPTS
SYSTEMATIC SOIL ANALYSIS . . .

Under a recent Government decree directed toward expanding the
Nation's agricultural production to maximum levels by rationalized
application of fertilizer, German farmers are required, upon request,
to submit to the competent soil-analysis authorities, samples of their
farm soil for analysis, according to a report received in the Office of
Foreign Agricultural Relations.

In general, ordinary crop farmers with a minimum of 5 hectares
(12.5 acres), and garden farmers with a minimum area of 1 hectare (2.5
acres), of cultivated soil, will be called upon to supply soil speci-
mens. One or more samples may be required, according to the needs for
testing of the particular soil, as ascertained by the authorities.

Farmers will be charged a fee of 0.50 mark (20 cents) for each
soil test, but total fees may not exceed 1.00 mark per hectare (16
cents per acre). Insufficient revenue from the fees for covering the
total cost of the soil-testing program will be compensated from Government funds.

The soil tests will be carried on throughout Germany upon a
comprehensive scale and are expected to yield scientific data re-
garding the precise fertilizer requirements of agricultural lands so
that commercial fertilizer will be applied in exactly the required
amounts, the report states. The tests will be carried out by some 70
Government agricultural experimental stations situated throughout Germany. Each experimental station at the beginning of the campaign will
conduct some 25,000 soil tests annually, and the number of tests will be
increased to 100,000 per station annually later on, when the testing
campaign becomes well established.

The soil-testing program is considered an important factor in
Germany's wartime economy in enabling the expansion of the Nation's
agricultural production to maximum proportions and thus lessening the
effects of the Allied blockade upon the Nation's food supply, the report points out.

For conducting the soil tests, advanced methods have been developed
based upon the use of photo-electric cells and principles of spectral
analysis. By means of this advanced physical method, the tests can be
conducted rapidly and inexpensively by ordinary workers, dispensing with
the former need for tedious methods of chemical analysis by scientifically
trained personnel, it is concluded.

* * * * * *

Index